The Beekeepers of Honey

Somefun Muritala

All Rights Reserved

TABLE OF CONTENTS

Introduction

Biodiversity

Chapter Six

Intensive Farming Method

Chapter Seven

Decrease in Habitat

Chapter Eight

Global Warming and Changing Weather Patterns

Chapter Nine

Pollution

Chapter Ten

Measures to Protect Bee Colony

Chapter Eleven

Processing of Honey

Conclusion

Reference

INTRODUCTION

These terms, which come from the Latin apis, "bee" (cf. apiary), are often used to refer to beekeepers: honey farmers, apiarists, or, less frequently, apiculturists[1]. Someone who maintains honey bees in hives, boxes, or other containers is referred to as a beekeeper. Bees are not under the beekeeper's control. Beekeepers own the hives or boxes and any related equipment. There is no restriction on the bees' ability to forage or swarm away. The hive provides a clean, dark, and protected home for the bees, so they typically return to the beekeeper's facility.

A beekeeper's standard equipment includes a smoker to calm the swarm, a veil to shield the face, gloves for inexperienced beekeepers or those who are allergic to stings, the extractor, which is used to centrifuge the honey out of the cells; the uncapping knife, which is used to unlock the honey cells; and a blunt steel blade known as a hive tool, which is used to separate the frames and other hive elements for inspection.

CHAPTER ONE

BEE KEEPING

Most A. cerana races produce less honey for the beekeeper and are smaller than A. mellifera bees. They also create smaller colonies. As opposed to A. mellifera, A. cerana neither gathers nor utilizes propolis. Before A. mellifera was brought to Asia in the late 1800s, A. cerana was the only hive bee present in the continent. It had been raised in conventional hives made of logs, boxes, barrels, baskets, and ceramics from the first or second century a.d. in China and most likely since the 300s b.c. in the upper Indus basin, which is today in Pakistan.

The management of colonies is comparable, but the apiculturist must take precautions against colony absconding. From 30 to 75 percent of colonies in India may disappear every year. A colony needs a young queen and enough supplies of honey or syrup and pollen at all times to avoid this. When feeding syrup, extra caution is required to avoid thieving. Additionally, wasps and ants must be kept out of colonies.

Higher latitudes produce larger bees, and in Kashmir (at an elevation of 1500 meters and above), A. cerana is nearly as large as A. mellifera and comparable in other aspects (the colonies don't go away, for example.

CHAPTER TWO

POLLINATORS

Let's begin with the most well-known and significant function of bees, which is pollination. Three out of four crops that produce fruit or seeds for human consumption worldwide depend on pollinators like bees, according to the Food and Agriculture Organization of the United Nations report "Why Bees Matter." Additionally, pollinators support the production of 87 major crop varieties and have an impact on 35% of the world's agricultural area.

More than any other agricultural management technique, pollination is the single most important agricultural factor that affects crop yields globally. The fact that crops that rely on pollinators, like bees, generate between 235 billion and 577 billion USD annually in value globally serves to emphasize the significance of pollinators for livelihoods.

There are other pollinator species, but none are as effective as bees. When it comes to the variety of plants it can pollinate, no other insect can compare. To the extent that the pollination efforts of the common bee are responsible for about one out of every three bites of food that you consume. This is the reason why the reduction in species variety and bee population drops are so concerning. Food instability may result from our inability to successfully pollinate all the crops needed for food production without bees.

Not only do bees aid in the pollination of our crops, but a vast array of other plants and trees also rely on insect pollination. These plants feed birds and other wild creatures in addition to maintaining the health of ecosystems.

In actuality, about 90% of plant species depend on pollinators in order to reproduce. Pollination is the process by which pollinators move pollen from one flower to another, assisting plants in producing fruit (technically anything with seeds within, so that includes items we typically think of as vegetables, such cucumbers, green beans, and tomatoes). Around 200,000 distinct animal species are known to function as pollinators worldwide. Approximately 1,000 of these are invertebrates, such as flies, beetles, butterflies, moths, and bees, while the remaining are vertebrates, such as bats, birds, and tiny mammals. More than 180,000 distinct plant species rely on pollinators for their pollination needs.

Plants depend on pollinators to survive, and plants:
provide an abundance of fruits, vegetables, and nuts that account for half of our food supply.
Provide half of the world's oils, fibers, and other basic commodities, including cotton needed to create clothing.
are employed in the production of several medications.
Give wildlife sustenance and shelter.
Maintain clean waterways
Avoid soil erosion
generate the oxygen that we breathe.
Take up CO2 to mitigate climate change worldwide.

More than 1,200 crops are pollinated annually worldwide thanks to pollinators. Approximately 75%, or 87 out of the top 115 food crops, are dependent on pollinators. More than $217 billion and $24 billion, respectively, are contributed to the US and global economies each year by pollinators. The value of pollinator services in the United States would reach a staggering $40 billion if we took into account the indirect products of plants, such milk and beef from cows fed alfalfa.

One of the world's most common and effective pollination species is the honey bee. Honey bees significantly boost the likelihood that a plant will yield a fruit or vegetable, as they can visit over 2,000 blossoms in a single day on average.

CHAPTER THREE

NATIVE BEES AND THEIR ROLE

A fascinating fact about bees in North America is that there are about 4,000 different species. These bees come in a great variety, ranging from bumblebees to cuckoo bees. Although some are longer than an inch, others are about an eighth of an inch. Metallic green or blue, dark brown or black, striped red or orange, and so on are some of the color variations.

Because they are not domesticated or because some of them don't resemble "traditional" bees (fuzzy, black, and yellow), native bees are frequently disregarded. The honey bee and these other bees are both silent and hardworking pollinators of our crops; they are the original inhabitants of North America.

Although they may not receive much attention, native bees have a significant impact on both the environment and the economy. The value of the crop in the US that benefits from natural insect pollination exceeded $9 billion in 2009. Regretfully, native bees are having equal difficulties to honey bees. Numerous species are in danger of going extinct, and you can learn more about them here. In addition to harming managed honey bees, diseases, parasites, and inadequate nutrition from monoculture farms also affect wild bee populations.

According to a National Academy of Sciences research released last year, there may be a disappearance of wild bees in the Mississippi River Valley, the Central Valley of California, the Midwest's maize belt, and other important agricultural areas. Modeled bee abundance decreased across 23% of US land area between 2008 and 2013.
We need to come up with fresh, creative ideas now more than ever to save these national

treasures and maintain the ecosystem's equilibrium.

CHAPTER FOUR

ECONOMIC IMPORTANT

The administration and upkeep of honey bees in order to generate honey and beeswax is known as apiculture, or the beekeeping industry. Well-known goods produced by the sector include royal jelly, honey, bee pollen, beeswax, and bee venom, to mention a few. These goods made from bees have a wide range of applications. For instance, beeswax finds frequent usage in the pharmaceutical and cosmetic industries, pollen can be used as a nutritional supplement, and royal jelly has medical applications as well as being used as a home cure for viral illnesses.

A reduction in bee populations poses a serious threat to the sector and jeopardizes the jobs of individuals who work in apiculture.

CHAPTER FIVE

BIODIVERSITY

The term "biodiversity" describes the range of various species that may be found in a given geographic area. It is an important part of healthy ecosystems, which are necessary for the provision of key resources like the food and air we breathe.

Bees are essential to the preservation of biodiversity. They enhance plant species diversity, which in turn affects the variety of insects and animals in a particular habitat, by moving pollen from blossom to flower and fertilizing a vast array of plants and trees.

Most people know that bees are important for the pollination of flowers and plants, but bees are also crucial when it comes to the pollination of many tree species. We can enjoy summer fruits from many tree species thanks to the activities of bees in the early spring. They also contribute to the growth of healthy forests and woodland areas which house a multitude of different animal species.

Unfortunately, the largest danger to bees comes from human activity. Intense farming methods, habitat loss, climate change and altered weather patterns, pollution, and excessive pesticide use are all contributing factors to the recent decline in bee numbers worldwide. Let's go deeper into these variables and how they affect bee populations:

CHAPTER SIX

INTENSIVE FARMING METHOD

Agricultural practices are becoming increasingly intensive, or what is known as industrial agriculture, in an effort to better address the rising global food demand.

Both higher labor output and higher crop yields are pushed by industrial agriculture. Monoculture farming, or growing only one type of crop, and replacing natural ecosystems with artificial fertilizers, insecticides, and other non-natural solutions are two methods that can be used to achieve this.

Such approaches have the drawback of harming ecosystems and decreasing biodiversity. In addition to this, intensive agricultural practices have a host of other negative consequences, including elevated greenhouse gas emissions, spillovers, water contamination, and even food insecurity. All of this may have a negative impact on bee populations, as research directly links industrial farming methods to a decline in the variety and quantity of bee species. In fact, many of these kinds of farms depend on hiring commercial beekeepers to help pollinate their crops.

CHAPTER SEVEN

DECREASE IN HABITAT

Because of the destruction and modification of their habitat, changes in land use can have a substantial impact on bee numbers. In the same way that cities are increasing to accommodate expanding populations, agricultural land is spreading and intensifying to fulfill the rising demand for food. That being said, this implies that bee habitats such as meadows, hedgerows, and rural areas are becoming increasingly rare.

For instance, during the 1930s, 97% of wildflower meadows in the UK have entirely vanished. As a result, bee populations have decreased; in the UK, two species of bumblebee have gone extinct. Regrettably, bee populations around the world are facing a similar trend, therefore the issue is not unique to the UK.

CHAPTER EIGHT

GLOBAL WARMING AND CHANGING WEATHER PATTERNS

In addition to raising global temperatures, climate change is producing more frequent and severe weather events like heatwaves, cyclones, flooding, and droughts. Bee populations are under severe stress as a result of this. For instance, a bee's feeding schedule may be disturbed by intense rain, its habitat may be destroyed by floods, and its food sources may be destroyed by drought. In addition to this, illness and pests are spreading to previously uninfested areas due to shifting weather patterns. As a result, viruses and parasites like mites can infect bee hives.

Because of milder winters and greater spring temperatures, flowers are flowering earlier in the season, which is another issue brought on by the rise in global temperatures. The danger is that populations of bees may not be there to feast on them at the appropriate time.

CHAPTER NINE

POLLUTION

According to recent research, air pollution might cause pollinators—like bees—to lose their capacity to detect floral scents, perhaps resulting in a third less pollination. This is believed to be a major contributing factor to the global fall in bee numbers.

Pollution in the air affects the aroma molecules generated by flowers and plants, which is essential for bees to find food and carry out efficient foraging. Pollination is reduced because bees have a harder time finding these kinds of food sources due to the air pollution particles.

Pesticides

In conventional farming, weed management, insect control, and disease prevention are achieved through the use of pesticides on crops. Over a thousand different types of pesticides are used worldwide, and some of the more traditional ones—which are already prohibited in many nations—can even linger in the soil and water for many years after they are applied.

Pesticides are bad for our insect populations, especially bee populations, in addition to being bad for human health.

In addition to delaying growth and affecting bees' ability to navigate and reproduce correctly, pesticides can weaken bees' immune systems. The mixture of various poisons that bees encounter is much more dangerous and has led to a higher bee mortality rate, which exacerbates the situation.

CHAPTER TEN

MEASURES TO PROTECT BEE COLONY

What specific measures are being taken to safeguard bee populations, considering their critical role in maintaining our ecosystems and producing food? The good news is that bees' predicament is starting to catch the attention of governments and organizations worldwide.

The European Union and other international organizations are beginning to take measures to shield pollinators from the dangerous chemicals and insecticides used in industrial agriculture. For instance, three dangerous pesticide classes known as neonicotinoids that are known to endanger bee populations are prohibited throughout the European Union. Pollinator habitat conservation has received recognition from other major summits and agreements including the Convention on Biological Diversity.

Individual nations are also acting. For instance, the UK has a National Pollinator Strategy and a "Implementation Plan for the Healthy Bees Plan 2030" that outlines more than fifty steps that beekeepers, bee farmers, and the UK government should take to safeguard and improve the country's bee populations.

But pesticide use and intensive farming methods pose the greatest harm to bee numbers.

Furthermore, despite attempts to outlaw the use of more dangerous kinds, pesticides are still widely used in farming operations in the UK and other nations throughout the world.

i) Create a Bee garden

Bee habitats are in danger, as we've already mentioned. This is why you can contribute to giving them food and a secure place to reside by creating your own bee garden. Furthermore, window boxes, flower pots, and planters are all excellent options for growing the kinds of plants that bees like to thrive without taking up a lot of space. The most crucial factor to take into account is the kind of plants you choose to grow; you should choose a variety of plants that bloom from March to September and are rich in nectar and pollen.

ii) Avoid use of chemicals

Use of pesticides, herbicides, and synthetic fertilizers in your garden should be strictly avoided as these chemicals are detrimental to bee populations. Rather, choose organic goods and apply compost to help your plants and soil get healthier. Ladybugs and other insects are available for purchase to ward off pests.

iii) Trees planting

The importance of trees to bees is sometimes overlooked; in addition to nectar, bees also consume the blossoms on trees. Actually, trees—rather than flowers—provide the majority of the nectar that bees need. For this reason, adding trees to your landscape is really beneficial. Bees can find shelter in the hollow of the tree, and it not only supplies food but also materials for them to build their nests.

Don't worry if you can't plant trees yourself; you can still make a difference by volunteering at a local organization that plants trees.

iv) Assist a weary bee

A bee that appears to be exhausted and in need of assistance is likely to be slow-moving and listless if you find him on the ground. A small dose of sugar is necessary for a bee in this state. To give the tiny striped man a boost of vitality, combine a few teaspoons of white granulated sugar with a small amount of water and drizzle it over a flower or arrange it on a platter. Just let it rest and leave it alone after you've fed it the sugary juice. He should soon possess sufficient energy to depart!

As bees produce more fruits and vegetables and are vulnerable to chemicals and parasites like the Varroa mite, which is why organic honey is so difficult to locate.

As African Honey Bees (AHBs) spread over the Americas, beekeepers who were used to dealing with comparatively gentle and manageable European Honey Bees (EHBs) found it difficult to adjust to their defensive behavior, and many gave up on beekeeping altogether. The amount of honey produced decreased, and many nations started importing honey instead of exporting it. For instance, after AHBs arrived in the Yucatan peninsula of Mexico, where stingless bees (Melipona and Trigona) and EHBs were both widely used, beekeeping in both varieties drastically decreased.

Honey production rebounded in much of the Americas as new beekeepers acclimated to AHBs, especially in Brazil. It seems that Kerr's goal of increasing honey output in the New World tropics will be accomplished, as AHBs are already used for honey production in many places of the Americas where EHBs were useless.

CHAPTER ELEVEN

PROCESSING OF HONEY

The bees in a beekeeper's hive store honey in the combs of an upper honey box, which is taken out after it is full. There are a few different ways to remove bees off combs in the honey box: you can shake and brush the bees off the combs, use a bee-escape board to allow the bees to exit the honey box but not return, use a bee repellant, or blow the bees out of the boxes with a stream of air.

The combs used to make beeswax can also be used to sell honey. But because the bees must expend energy to make wax, honey yields are higher when the honey is taken and the combs are given back to the bees.

On the other hand, honey that is sold by the comb has the least changed flavor and is clearly unadulterated. These factors keep the market for comb honey alive. Comb honey can be made from bigger combs or in "sections" where the bees are given little wooden or plastic frames with a thin wax comb foundation on which to construct and fill cells. As "chunk honey," comb and extracted honey are occasionally mixed together in a jar.

The majority of honey is prepared without any comb or wax and separated from the wax comb in preparation for sale in containers.

In order to process honey, the following steps must be completed:

(1) removing bees from combs to be harvested and transporting them to the honey house;

(2) heating the combs to a temperature of 32 to 35°C;

(3) removing the wax cappings that the bees use to seal finished honey into the comb;

(4) extracting the honey from the combs using a centrifuge; and

(5) clarifying the honey through settling or filtration by running it through a strainer and/or

baffle tank. After that, the honey could undergo pressure filtering, heating to remove any crystals, and increasing the shelf life and purity of the liquid. You can add seed crystals if you want a consistent granulated honey.

CHAPTER TWELVE

Botanical and Geographic Origins of Honey: Chemical Composition, Characterization, and Differentiation

Pure honeys are relatively expensive. In order to boost the honey's sweetness, some beekeepers may feed their hives with illegal sweets. Adding sugar directly to items made with honey is another illegal activity. A variety of sweeteners have been employed, such as molasses, corn syrups, maple syrup, cane sugar, beet sugar, and acid/inverted sugar syrups.

Honey typically has a water content of less than 20%. Via vacuum evaporation or centrifugation, any extra water can be eliminated.

Artificial water addition to honeys may result in honey fermentation. The Eastern Apicultural Society of North America recommends that honey have a water content of between 15.5% and 18.6%, which is considered a reasonable range. It is improbable that highly diluted honey can be used for adulteration. The natural water content of honey can range from 13.6% to 23%, depending on the honey's origin, weather, and other elements. When the water content of honey is less than 18%, fermentation normally does not become an issue.

CHAPTER THIRTEEN

COLONY COLLAPSE DISORDER

Commercial honey beekeepers in the USA started to experience significant bee losses around 2005, and these colony losses persisted every year after that. The condition was originally referred to as "The law of thirds: one third dead, one third weak, and one third fine" by a beekeeper. A novel illness called colony collapse disorder (CCD), which is not always contagious, has been linked to this high death rate.

The symptoms of the disease are as follows:

(1) a rapid loss of adult worker bees, meaning that adult numbers decline over a few weeks, but not with the sudden mortality that is typically observed with pesticide poisonings;

(2) the colony is rapidly dying, but only a few or no dead bees are found in or around the hive;

(3) a small cluster of adult bees with an egg-laying queen and brood; or

(4) the colony is dead, but it has brood and honey and pollen stores intact, and there has been no invasion by hive pests like wax moths (Cox-Foster et al., 2007). As of this writing, no one parasite, pathogen, or toxin has been identified that can completely account for the origin of this disease.

An investigation into potential infections or parasites that could be connected to the frequency of CCD was conducted in 2006 using a metagenomic survey of bees from various US states. An Israeli virus recently identified as the Israeli acute paralysis virus (IAPV, Table 12.2) (Cox-Foster et al., 2007) was the only pathogen detected in all the CCD samples and none of the non-CCD samples. It was unknown that IAPV existed in the USA at the time of that study, but subsequent research has demonstrated that it has existed since at least 2002 (Chen and Evans, 2007).

Whether IAPV causes CCD has not yet been established. Beekeepers in Europe have also witnessed significant losses of honey bees; some scientists attribute these losses to the introduction of N. ceranae (see Section 12.3.4), while others believe that a combination of variables, such as long-term chemical exposure, may be at play.

As Chen and Huang (2010) point out, N. ceranae is now widely distributed in the USA; yet, the metagenomic survey did not find a significant correlation between the pathogen and CCD.

Furthermore, a novel undescribed iridovirus and N. ceranae co-infection have been suggested as the causes of CCD (Bromenshenk et al., 2010). Previous descriptions of an iridovirus from A. cerana have been published, but not from A. mellifera (Bailey et al., 1976; Bailey and Ball, 1978; Verma and Phogat, 1982). Therefore, more research is required to validate the virus's occurrence in this host as well as in the USA.

Despite quantifying over 200 variables, a comprehensive epidemiological approach was used in the USA in 2009 to determine the cause of CCD; however, no single factor was able to be established as the origin of this condition.

Nevertheless, low coumaphos levels in the hive did match up with CCD, even though the degree of varroa mite infestation was not a reliable indicator (vanEngelsdorp et al., 2009, 2010). According to van Engelsdorp et al. (2010), two other pesticides were also shown to be predictive of the prevalence of CCD. However, the authors did not state whether the incidence of CCD was associated with high or low levels of these pesticides.

The United States of America carried out a highly comprehensive and broad investigation of the levels of pesticide contamination in honey bees and honey bee colonies in the 2000s (Mullin et al., 2010).

High quantities of tau-fluvalinate and coumaphos have been detected in almost all American honey bee colonies. Low pesticide levels can have unanticipated, long-term, or delayed impacts on bees, as previously described (see Section

12.3.7). This survey found that a wide range of insecticides, miticides, and fungicides are present in honey bee environments. It is unclear if poisonings have a part in CCD, but the effect of pesticide exposure—especially exposures below the acute toxicity levels—deserves more research.

According to extensive yearly studies of both commercial and hobbyist beekeepers in the United States, over 30% of all colonies perish in the winter (van Engelsdorp et al., 2008, 2010, 2011). CCD is not the most common reason, though. The most common reasons given by beekeepers for their winter colony losses were weather, varroa mites, queen failure, and malnutrition (particularly among hobbyist beekeepers). Consequently, even while it's possible that honey bee colony losses are increasing globally (IBRA, 2010), CCD isn't the direct cause of this increase—but it is undoubtedly a contributing component.

As previously demonstrated, CCD is a complex illness with a lack of clarity. Though the above-described symptoms have been identified by a group of experts as indicative of CCD, the symptoms are not definitive and could stem from a variety of conditions. Because of this, there is disagreement among bee researchers regarding whether CCD is a distinct disease, with some proposing that it is a group of symptoms with multiple potential causes, such as infections with N. ceranae, infestations with varroa mites, and abiotic factors like prolonged exposure to pesticides (Anderson and East, 2008).

Based on firsthand knowledge (R. R. James), professional beekeepers and apiary inspectors apply a sweeping interpretation to any significant losses they encounter, even in cases where they can positively identify the source (e.g., a varroa mite infestation or pesticide exposure). For instance, one commercial beekeeper in the same area said that pesticide poisoning was the primary cause of "his" CCD, whereas another apiary inspector claimed that varroa mites were the main cause of CCD in his area (R. R. James, unpubl.).

Beekeepers' imprecise definition of CCD makes it challenging to analyze their records and surveys. The circumstances could be comparable to those of the Isle of Wight sickness in the British Isles as reported by Bailey and Ball (1991):

"Bee deaths can occur for a variety of reasons other than infections, and it's highly likely that non-infectious disease-related deaths among bee deaths frequently contributed to the Isle of Wight disease's death toll." At the time, the belief that Isle of Wight disease was, in fact, contagious led to the conclusion that tracheal mites were the source of the illness, a finding that several scientists contested (Bailey and Ball, 1991). Since it can be highly challenging to identify the cause of a colony's death, a variety of mortalities are frequently included as CCD, which makes it more difficult to identify the true cause.

Novel aspects of self-employment to promote sustainability in an evolving world

Using the previously indicated methods, honey refining, processing, and packaging facilities get in direct contact with forward-thinking beekeepers to purchase honey.

Pharmaceutical companies buy other goods including propolis, bee pollen, and royal jelly because they have innovative uses in medicine (Kaur, Kumar, & Harjai, 2020). Beeswax is used in the candle, crayon, and polish industries.

Craftsmen can obtain employment by creating affordable hives, contemporary hives, and beekeeping supplies for beekeepers.

CHAPTER FOURTEEN

GOVERNMENT INITIATIVE PROGRAM

1.

In order to guarantee the quality of the honey, beekeepers should receive training on practices such as separating ripe honey from combs containing unripe honey, pollen, and brood, as well as utilizing a honey extractor and clean containers.

2.

Organize efforts to raise awareness among bee keepers, merchants, and marketers about the needs of the evolving honey and bee wax markets.

3.

Supplying beekeepers and honey traders with basic equipment for harvesting, processing, and storage.

CHAPTER FIFTEEN

THE GENETIC STRUCTURE OF HONEYBEE REPRODUCTION

With the possible exception of stinging behavior, the beekeeper does not value the output of any one employee. Honey and wax production, as well as pollination efficiency, are the two commercially significant characteristics of honeybees that are examined at the colony level. Distinctive characteristics like resilience to illness, capacity for overwintering, and propensity to swarm are mostly noteworthy due to their impact on the main characteristics or ability to avert colony collapse.

The only person in a colony who can be said to be of long-lasting significance is the queen, but she has no direct control over any of the major characteristics; instead, her pheromones, the genes she passes on to the worker population, and the eggs she produces all have an impact on these traits. As a result, breeders frequently handle a colony as a single unit. Colony-level features are undoubtedly the most important biological level in terms of commerce out of all of them.

The social architecture of a colony is shaped by various factors that influence its performance, including the genes inherited by its members, the relational ties between individuals within and across castes, and the various biological levels of organization that result from the colony's multiple generations.

CHAPTER SIXTEEN

ALLERGIES TO INSECTS THAT STING

The greater the number of stings, the higher the chance of acquiring a sting allergy. If two stings happen in a short amount of time, like a few weeks to two months, the likelihood is much higher. On the other hand, beekeepers who experience fewer than ten stings annually are far more likely to get SR than those who experience more than 200 stings.

More severe sting reactions are linked to cardiovascular disorders and their treatment with β-blocking medications and ACE inhibitors; occasionally, these medications can also cause long-term morbidity from cardiac or cerebrovascular infarction as a result of anaphylaxis.

But overall, the risk of systemic sting reactions is not increased by β-blockers. An increased baseline blood tryptase level, which is a sign of systemic mastocytosis, increases the likelihood of severe or even fatal systemic sting reactions. Patients with a sting allergy to Hymenoptera do not experience a higher incidence of atopy than the general public. Conversely, systemic reactions may be more severe and more frequently affect the respiratory tract in an atopic patient with a venom allergy to Hymenoptera. Bettors who are venomous are about 50% atopic. During their labor on the beehives, atopic beekeepers may also get sensitized by breathing in venomous dust.

Artificial feeding of bees during nectar flow

In periods of the year when the beehive does not receive natural nectar income, supplemental (also known as artificial) feeding of honeybees with sugar syrups is a standard and essential management activity. Beekeepers that feed their bees near or during a nectar flow need to exercise extra caution in order to prevent contaminating honey with these syrups. Even though it's not the most common method of adulterating honey, improper artificial bee feeding practices can contaminate honey with sugar syrups.

To distinguish between deliberate honey adulteration and inadvertent small contamination of honey with ingredients used for supplemental feeding, it is recommended that any technology used to detect honey adulteration provide a threshold of around 5% tolerance.

CHAPTER SEVENTEEN

ARTIFICIAL INSEMINATION

Honey bee artificial insemination (AI) has developed into a highly successful and often used technique in less than a century since Watson's groundbreaking experiments, particularly in research. Nonetheless, there is still a limited adoption of AI among beekeepers, at least anecdotally. If there weren't so many obstacles in the way of the technique's wider adoption, it would be more widespread. To better understand the adoption hurdles, research is required to examine how beekeepers perceive and respond to AI and other breeding technologies. Then, more general inquiries about adoption rate and the perceived financial and genetic benefits for operators can be addressed. It should be feasible to incorporate AI into the beekeeping sector more fully by providing answers to these issues.

It is important to compare AI's performance to that of the natural mating system while evaluating its effectiveness. More than 90% of inseminated queens live to lay fertilized eggs, which is comparable to the survival percentage of spontaneously mated queens in breeding operations (Moritz and Kühnert, 1984). The literature comparing spontaneously mated and artificially matched queens across variables including lifetime and colony productivity has already been evaluated by Cobey (2007). Her review's comparisons show that natural mating and artificial insemination have about identical success rates.

CONCLUSION

In the United States, honey bees are the most often utilized species for commercial pollination. In addition to managing and pollinating more than 100 crops cultivated in North America, they boost the US economy annually by $15 billion. Over 90% of the pollination of several crops, like almonds, which bring $4.8 billion to the US economy annually, is done by honey bees. However, honey bees do more than just pollinate crops; they also pollinate native and wild plants, which adds to all the advantages for the environment and society that pollinators generally are associated with.

REFERENCES

1.

Insect Pathology (Second Edition), Rosalind R.
James, Zengzhi Li, 2012.

2. http://www.planetbee.org

3. Published in Advances in Animal Experimentation and Modeling, 2022 by Ranbir Chander Sobti,... Anudeep

4. Clinical Immunology (Fourth Edition), Ulrich R. Müller,... Arthur Helbling, 2013.

5. Encyclopedia of Insects (Second Edition), Eva Crane and P. Kirk Visscher, 2009.

6. In Advances in Insect Physiology, edited by Benjamin P. Oldroyd and Peter R. Oxley, 2010.